Done in a Day

Easy detailing and weathering projects for your model railroad

By Pelle K. Søeborg

KALMBACH BOOKS

Published by Kalmbach Publishing Co., 21027 Crossroads Circle, Waukesha, WI 53186.

Visit our website at: www.Kalmbach.com/Books

Printed in the United States of America.

13 12 11 10 09   2 3 4 5 6

Photos: Portrait on page 4 by Claus Løgstrup. All other photos by Pelle K. Søeborg.
Layout and design: Pelle K. Søeborg (www.soeeborg.dk).

Publisher's Cataloging-In-Publication Data
Søeborg, Pelle K.   Done in a day : easy detailing and weathering projects for your model railroad /

by Pelle K. Søeborg
     p. : ill. ; cm.
   Includes index.

   ISBN: 978-0-89024-762-4
I. Railroads—Models--Finishing--Handbooks, manuals, etc. I. Title. II. Title: Easy detailing and weathering projects for your model railroad
TF197 .S639 2009
625.1/9

Contents

Pelle K. Søeborg

. . . is a designer with his own graphics business in Farum, Denmark. In the early '90s, Pelle began to pick up issues of *Model Railroader,* and he has been a model railroader ever since. A trip to the United States in 1992 added to his interest in modeling United States prototypes.

Pelle has written a number of articles for *Model Railroader* throughout the years and has provided photos for model train calendars, Woodland Scenics, and Walthers catalogues. His book about his home layout, *Mountain to Desert: Building the HO Scale Danville and Donner River,* was published by Kalmbach Books in 2006.

Preface

Since my entry into the hobby in the early 1990s, the focus in the hobby has changed. If you compare an out-of-the-box locomotive model of today with a model made just 15 years ago, it is obvious that the model from the past needs a lot of work to appear as detailed as the present-day model. When I needed a new locomotive for my railroad, I used to start out with an undecorated Athearn locomotive kit, which back then was a good starting point. I replaced the molded grab irons with wire parts. The cab and sometimes the nose were replaced with better-looking parts from Cannon & Co. On some of my older Athearn locomotives, I also replaced the molded fans with see-through versions. Air and m.u. hoses, snow plows, fuel tank, lift rings, and other details were also applied to the model. The model then went to the paint shop to receive the appropriate paint scheme. It definitely required some modeling skills to make a good model of a specific prototype back then.

Today most of that is not needed. Many current locomotive models already have the correct details for specific railroads. Separately applied wire grab irons, plows, hoses, see-through fans, and fuel tank details are common. The paint and lettering are usually precise. The same improvements are also seen on rolling stock.

In many ways, this development is a good thing. However, many of us who find pleasure in making realistic-looking models still want to be able to say "I made this" rather than "I bought this." The good thing is that all the modeling time we used to spend on detailing locomotives and cars can be spent on other aspects of the hobby. I for one turned my attention toward making scenery, weathering locomotives and rolling stock, and building loads for my freight cars. All of this has resulted in practicing my modeling skills by building a more realistic-looking model railroad. If the models had not improved as they have, I would probably be spending most of my hobby time detailing and painting locomotives.

Another part of the model railroad hobby that has gone through an even larger development—a revolution really—is control. I am thinking of Digital Command Control. The step from analog to DCC operations was enormous, and DCC made it possible to run trains in a much more realistic way. I clearly remember how impressed I was with the early two-digit-address decoders with only a few available functions. Now all my locomotives have sound decoders with four-digit addresses and more available functions than I will ever use. I can only imagine what DCC will look like ten years from now. We will probably wonder how we could have lived with the primitive decoders of today with all their limitations.

There is no doubt that the evolution of the model railroad hobby will continue, but some things will never change. There will always be room for practicing your modeling skills in one way or another.

—Pelle K. Søeborg

This weathering on this string of freight cars was accomplished in a couple of Sunday afternoons.

Introduction

In my hobby cabinet, I always like to keep a few of what I call Sunday afternoon projects. These are fun self-assignments that take no longer than an afternoon or two to finish. Most involve freight cars or locomotives that need weathering, but they could also include projects such as modeling freight loads or adding sound to a locomotive.

In this book, I have detailed in text and pictures a selection of projects you can complete on your own by simply looking over my shoulder.

Weathering rolling stock

Before any new freight car or locomotive hits the rails on my private model railroad, the Daneville & Donner River, it receives some degree of weathering. It may seem obvious, but how much weathering I give my models depends on the age of the prototype. Models representing older freight cars usually receive a heavier weathering than models representing newer cars.

This rule does not apply to locomotives. Sometimes older locomotives are repainted and may appear just as shiny and clean as newer locomotives. Most lo-

comotives start their lives on my layout relatively clean with only a light weathering. After a couple of years they receive a second and heavier weathering and become classified as older locomotives.

Freight cars are rarely repainted, and as a rule, the older they are, the more rusty and filthy they appear. I have freight cars on my layout that have received a second weathering just as my locomotives have, but this is more the exception than the rule.

Collecting prototype info

I use field trips to take photos of prototypes both for inspiration and for accu-

racy when I sit down to weather my models. My intention is not to make an exact copy of the weathered appearance of a specific prototype but to use the pictures as general guide for how different types of rolling stock age.

Take pictures of common freight cars and locomotives the next time you are railfanning. The photos will give you the information you need for your next weathering project. One angle that's especially difficult to photograph is train roofs. We do not normally see car and locomotive roofs as we watch trains, but it's one of the most common views on layouts. Use every chance you have to take pictures above trains and capture roof detail.

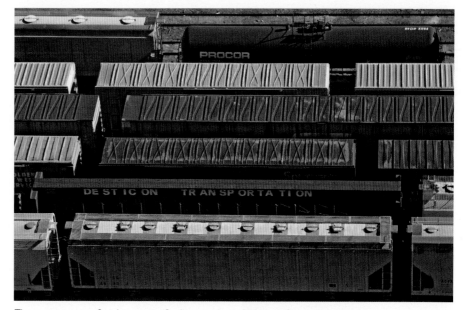

These prototype freight car roofs show various degrees of rust and wear.

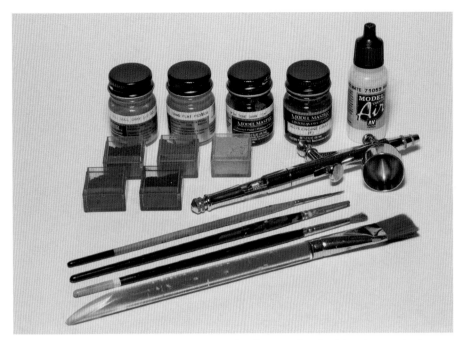

This is all you need to start weathering: an airbrush, a couple of soft brushes, and a fine hard brush. My preferred type of paint for weathering is Model Master's solvent-based paint in Flat Gull Gray, Sand, Dark Skin Tone, and Engine Gray. The colors of the powdered chalks I use are Light Rust, Medium Rust, Dark Rust, Brown, and Black.

I made this simple jig to hold models while weathering them from a wood block and pieces of bent piano wire. I drilled a series of holes in the wood block into which I can stick the wires according to the length of the model.

The wires can swing from side to side. This way I am able to fine-tune the space in between them. The wire is stuck in the screw hole in the freight car's bolster. The white styrene tube around the wire will prevent the model from sliding down no matter how deep the screw hole is.

Weathering techniques

Weathering is essential to make freight cars or locomotives look realistic, yet many modelers seem intimidated by the prospect of ruining their new rolling stock. There is nothing complicated in the techniques I use. Even if you have never weathered a freight car or locomotive, I am confident you can accomplish a satisfying result by following these instructions.

My weathering technique is a combination of airbrushing and the application of powdered chalks. I use the airbrush to tone down the model's bright colors and to apply an even layer of road grime to the lower area of the model.

The powdered chalks are used for creating rust spots, streaking dirt down the sides, adding soot around the exhaust, and for other spot effects.

Tools for weathering

You will need an airbrush. I prefer a dual-action airbrush with a top-mounted color cup. With a dual-action airbrush, you can control both the air and color flow via one lever. This is an advantage if you want to vary the spray on specific areas on a model rather than simply applying a solid one-color coat.

You will also need an assortment of various paint brushes such as a fine brush for paint and a couple of soft brushes for applying powdered chalks.

A jig for holding models during the weathering process is absolutely necessary. With your model safely in the jig, you can work hands-free and avoid fingerprints and other blemishes. I have made a simple but effective version from a block of wood and piano wire.

Paint for weathering

Most of the paint I use for weathering is thinned to a wash before it is applied. My preferred type of paint for weathering is Model Master's solvent-based paint.

Solvent-based paint leaves an even dusty look. Acrylic paint thinned to a wash leaves a coarser pattern. The colors I use are mainly limited to Flat Gull Gray, Sand, Dark Skin Tone, and Engine Gray.

Gull Gray has a warm light gray color, which I primarily use for fading the roofs on diesel locomotives.

Sand has a light grey beige color well suited for fading all types of colored surfaces.

Dark Skin Tone is a dark brown color looking very much like the road grime seen along the lower area of the car and locomotive sides and ends. Everywhere under the train will also be covered by this road grime.

Engine Gray has an almost-black dark gray tone. Mixed with Dark Skin Tone, it is the perfect color for painting black weathered freight car trucks. After the weathering is applied, I seal it with clear flat varnish to withstand handling.

My preferred varnish is Vallejo Model Air Matte Varnish and Satin Varnish. These are acrylic varnishes that dry in 15 minutes or less.

With most types of paint, the color pigment has a tendency to stick to the bottom of the bottle as a paste that can be difficult to dissolve even if you shake it for a long time. Place a little steel ball in the paint bottle. When you shake it, the ball will loosen the pigment and return your paint to a proper consistency.

Airbrushing rules

There are a few, but important, rules you should remember when using an airbrush. To obtain an even, smooth layer of paint, you'll need to start the spray off the model, then move to the model. Similarly, do not stop until the spray has passed the entire model. Move the airbrush with a steady, even motion and maintain the same distance to the model.

The air pressure needs to be adjusted depending on the type of paint. Water-based paints (acrylics) normally require a higher pressure than solvent-based paint. For solvent-based paint I operate with a setting of 20-25 psi of pressure and 25-30 psi for water-based paint.

It is not difficult to use an airbrush, but if you have never tried it, I recommend not weathering your best freight cars. Practice on an old one first to get the feel of it.

The next important rule is to clean your airbrush immediately after use. This is critical when using water-based paint. Unlike solvent-based paint, water-based paint can't be dissolved after it has dried. I use common window cleaning fluid as airbrush cleaner after I have sprayed with acrylic paint.

Powdered chalks

Powdered chalks or weathering powders are dry color pigments. They are applied with a soft brush with a technique very similar to applying make-up. Be aware that powdered chalks act differently on light surfaces than on a dark surfaces, so practice on a small area of each model.

The colors of the powdered chalks I use are Light Rust, Medium Rust, Dark Rust, Brown, and Black. With these five colors you can weather almost any type of rolling stock.

Traces of spilled contents on tank cars are easily copied with a fine brush and some black acrylic hobby paint.

Creating patched road numbers is an interesting modeling project. These cars probably have a new owner and had to be renumbered.

If you model contemporary railroads as I do, you can't ignore graffiti. This hopper has been patched to cover old graffiti just to be vandalized again.

On remote sidings, you may be lucky to find old freight cars from fallen-flag railroads.

Here's a good example of a weathered boxcar. The paint appears to have been bleached by the sun revealing plenty of rust spots.

This old Soo Line boxcar has seen better days. You'll need plenty of rust-colored powder to make a replica of such extreme weathering.

Auto racks always seem to develop rusted roofs as they get older. Note how nice and clean the Union Pacific car (right) is in comparison.

This close-up shows how grimy, rusty, and dirty freight car trucks become after countless miles on the tracks.

See how the rust from the roof has been washed down the sides on this SP auto rack.

After years of exposure to sun, rain, and snow, black tank cars turn many shades of gray and brown.

In this era of mergers, you can find locomotives in fallen-flag paint schemes showing temporary patches with their new owners' logos and road numbers. It's fun to update one of your older locomotives the same way.

It's not just freight cars that are painted with graffiti. It occasionally happens to locomotives too. I wonder how many spray cans it took to paint this Union Pacific engine in Mojave, California.

Traces of a fire in the engine compartment would be a nice feature on a scale model.

The view of the roofs of these Union Pacific locomotives clearly shows the sooted area around the exhaust stack.

If you favor extreme weathering, this Santa Fe Dash 8-40CW could be a great project..

Loads for open freight cars: Another great use for a couple of Sunday afternoons.

Loads for open freight cars

I have a passion for open freight cars with loads, and I've finally assembled a small fleet of flat cars and gondolas for which I have been seeking suitable loads. Although freight car loads are available—both as kits and ready-made—I have had difficulty finding realistic-looking loads that suit my needs. That led me to start making my own loads, which turned out to be a rewarding part of my modeling. On my rail fan trips, I take pictures of interesting loads, which I then try to re-create in HO scale.

It has become a sport for me to find materials for making specific loads, and my research has taken me to hobby shops other than train stores. I found many useful materials in a store specializing in RC cars and airplanes. I've also found materials I could use in building-supply stores.

Pipes make excellent loads for open freight cars, and as you can see, they show up on flat cars as well as in gondolas.

Turn a shiny new boxcar
into rolling stock long past its prime

This project describes how to create a weathered look to a boxcar using thin coats of paint applied with an airbrush and applying powdered chalks with soft brushes to a brand new InterMountain unit.

If you study your prototype photos, I bet you will notice that the common boxcar red on many older cars has been bleached by the sun. And if you could get up high, you would notice rust has attacked the roofs of many.

Along the lower area of the car sides and ends you'll find a layer of brake-shoe dust and dirt, which is whipped up from the roadbed in the slipstream of the train.

The entire underside of the carbody is covered by road grime. This rusty, grimy, streaky look is exactly what we're after.

Preparing the model

I separated the trucks from the underbody and remove the wheelsets. If the couplers are easy to remove, you should do that also. If not, then it's a good idea to cover them with masking tape.

You do not want any paint to get into the axle bearings in the truck side frames. I have a couple of freight cars suffering from that problem. They run as if their brakes were on all the time, almost needing to be pulled down a 2.5 percent grade!

A simple way to cover the axle bearings is to replace the car's wheel set with another set. I have a dozen pairs of wheels I use for that purpose. Another way is applying a protective dab of liquid mask in each of the holes.

Wipe the carbody clean of fingerprints and dust. Even if it is a new car from an unopened box, there may be fingerprints on the shell left by the person who assembled or packed it. I normally use a clean, dry piece of cloth. If you light the boxcar from an angle, you can usually spot any fingerprints or residue left on the body. When the parts are clean, handle them with gloves on.

Fading the paint

Place the boxcar in your spray booth or in a well-ventilated area (many modelers use a garage or even paint outdoors to be safe from fumes). Here, I placed the boxcar in my homemade jig. I filled the airbrush with Model Master Sand thinned to a wash and gave the boxcar sides a couple of light coats. The roof received a couple of coats of Gull Gray also thinned to a wash.

As I mentioned in the last chapter, I prefer solvent-based paint for this as it leaves an even dusty look. I take very close-up photography of my model trains, and dots of paint from coarse-grained acrylics can show up. Let the paint dry for an hour or so before you move on.

Modernizing with yellow reflective stripes

I decided to update this boxcar with the yellow reflective stripes you see on many freight cars today.

The stripe is from a BNSF diesel decal sheet. I cut the stripe in appropriate pieces, dipped them in water, and applied them to the body with a little Microset decal softening fluid. When I was satisfied with their location I brushed them with a little Solvaset and left them to dry.

Creating a rusty roof

There are several ways to recreate heavy buildups of rust. Some modelers simply paint it on, but you can also use powdered chalks, which leave a textured surface very similar to real rust.

You will need a wet base where you want the rust powder to adhere. I used a flat clear varnish. I brush the varnish on an area and immediately apply the powder directly on the wet area. On larger areas,

This nice clean boxcar from InterMountain will soon be transformed into an old rusty freight hauler with many years of hard service behind it.

The first step is to tone down the original paint. This is accomplished by airbrushing the body with a grayish beige color, thinned to a wash.

I apply the powder with a homemade shaker. On smaller areas, I dab it on it with a soft brush.

On this car, I used two shades of rust—dark and medium. Old rust appears dark reddish-brown, while new rust is more orange. I randomly apply the shades using photos to suggest where old and new rust might live.

I let the rust-colored powdered chalks that have been applied on wet varnish sit for five to ten minutes before wiping off any excess powder with a wide brush. This leaves the varnished area covered with a solid layer of rust and the rest of the roof

I updated this car by applying yellow reflective stripes, which came from a Microscale decal sheet for BNSF diesels.

Applying the powdered chalks

Severe rust attacks start with clear flat varnish. I didn't apply varnish to the entire area where I wanted rust but only to a third of the area. If you apply it to too large of an area, there is a risk that the varnish will dry before you have the chance to apply the powder.

Apply the powdered chalks while the varnish is still wet. You can use a soft brush to push the powder into the varnish. Randomly shake on different shades of rust. Old rust has a dark brown-red color, and new rust is more orange.

Let the powdered chalks sit for five to ten minutes before you brush off excess powder with a wide soft brush. This leaves a transparent layer of rust on the rest of the roof just like the traces from rust washed down by the rain. Give the entire roof some black powder to age everything.

The carbody also needs to be treated with powdered chalks. The rust here is in much smaller areas and more scattered. I dabbed small spots on and around the doors with clear varnish and applied rust-colored powder on the wet varnish with a soft brush.

Excess rust powder is brushed off with strokes directed downward. Black powder helps blend everything. The black on the sides comes from soot and dirt washed down from the roof by the rain so I always move the brush in the same direction, downward.

Along the lower areas on the sides will be a layer of grimy dust. This is applied with an airbrush. I use Model Master Dark Skin Tone, a dark gray-brown. I thin the paint to a wash and apply several coats to the lower areas of the carbody. Finally everything is sealed with a coat of flat clear varnish.

The boxcar has been changed into a weather-beaten, rusty old freight car. Note the realistic appearance of the built-up rust on the roof in the photo at right.

After the trucks were painted with a grimy black, they received a little rust-colored powder. In the photo below, you can see the finished truck with wheelsets in place, which first were painted with a grimy brown and then treated with rust-colored powder.

with a less-opaque layer of rust just as if the rain has washed rust away from the rusted areas down the roof. Finally the roof received some black powder to give it a more aged look.

The car sides received smaller rust attacks—especially at the doors—along with some black powder applied randomly with a wide brush.

The lower area of the body and the underside were sprayed with a gray brown color to simulate the grime and brake-shoe dust, which always will be present on these areas.

The trucks were first airbrushed with grimy black paint. When the paint was dry, I applied a little rust-colored powder to them. The wheels were brush-painted with a brownish gray. When they were dry, I applied some rust-colored powder to them.

Finally the carbody and trucks were sealed with clear flat varnish to withstand handling.

Boxcar gallery

This Milwaukee Road boxcar has been weathered using the same techniques described in this chapter, that is, rust-colored powder on wet varnish. The rust is much more visible on a yellow surface than on a brown boxcar.

The green on this Hutchinson Northern boxcar has been faded, and spots of rust have been applied to the body, especially on and around the doors. The next chapter shows how to create the look of the patched road numbers. The graffiti is a Blair Line decal. The tags were painted with a fine brush.

This Golden West boxcar has been given a bleached appearance with oversprays of thinned gray-beige. Note the road grime along the lower area of the carbody.

Add graffiti and tags: A completely legal way to vandalize a covered hopper

Like it or not, graffiti has become a permanent part of the contemporary railroad scene. If you model the present time as I do, you have to apply graffiti to at least a few of your freight cars for your layout to be realistic. Applying graffiti is made easy by Blair Line, whose graffiti decals are replicas of real graffiti.

Tags—the scribbles—are signatures made by graffiti painters or street gangs. You have to paint on tags by hand with a fine brush. A permanent ink marker can also do the job.

Before getting started, this Atlas hopper needs to be prepared. Wipe the body clean of fingerprints, residue, and dust with a dry piece of cloth. Separate the trucks from the body and the wheels from the trucks.

On some freight cars, the area with the road numbers has been patched. This could be because the car was renumbered recently or perhaps the original numbers became unreadable. If you want to replicate such a patch, simply cover the area you want patched with masking tape before you start the weathering process. Leave the mask on till you are finished, and the area will look newly painted when the masking is removed again.

The hopper has to go through the same basic steps as the boxcar in the previous chapter beginning with toning down the original color. As the color of the car-body already is light, the usual sand color will be too dark. Instead I mixed a little Gull Gray in flat white and gave the hopper a couple of light coats. Remember the color needs to be thinned to a wash.

Creating rust spots

As described in the previous chapter, an effective way to create rust attacks is by applying clear varnish to the areas you want rusted and then dab rust-colored powdered chalks on the wet varnish. The hopper received some rust spots on the side as if something had hit it and scratched the paint. I also gave it a little rust in the corners.

Applying the overall grime and dirt

A little bit of the chalk goes a long way as the colored power is much more visible on a lighter gray surface than on brown or black surfaces.

I applied rust, brown, and black powdered chalks to the carbody with a wide soft brush. Each time I dipped the brush in powder, I made one or two strokes on a sheet of paper to get rid of most of the powder before turning to the hopper. It is easier to control the amount of powder on the car with several light coats than with one heavy coat. Be sure to brush vertically, starting from the top of the car and moving toward the bottom when applying the powders.

When I was satisfied with the look, I carefully removed the masking tape from the patched areas. The body was ready to receive a coat of flat varnish to seal the powdered chalks and create a smooth surface for the graffiti decals.

Tag your trains

Start by cutting out the graffiti decals you want on your car. Trim off as much of the clear decal film as you can so only the printed area remains.

Dip the decal in water and wait a few minutes till you can slide the decal off the backing paper. Apply some decal setting solution to the area where you want to place the decal on the freight car. Slide the decal onto the carbody and place it in position. If it doesn't move easily, apply more setting solution.

When the decal is properly placed, apply a little Solvaset on it. Solvaset softens

Here's the Atlas hopper before it was turned into a target for graffiti painters.

First, masking tape was applied over a few markings as a "resist" to the weathering techniques to follow. This will result in shiny new areas replicating patched markings.

To fade the main lettering, the carbody was airbrushed with a flat light gray thinned to a wash. This coat left a flat surface perfect for applying powders.

Applying the basic weathering

I started by making scattered rust spots on the carbody. The spots start as dabs of flat varnish applied with a fine brush.

Rust-colored powdered chalks were applied to the still-wet varnish. I let the powder sit for a couple of minutes before I blew loose powder away.

Brush the excess powder on the varnish spots downward to make it look like rain has washed rust down the side of the car.

I then "painted" the carbody with rust, brown, and black powdered chalks. The powders will show more on a light surface than it would on boxcar red, so I wiped most of the powder off the brush before turning to the car. It is easier to control the amount of powder applied to the body by giving it several light layers than one heavy layer.

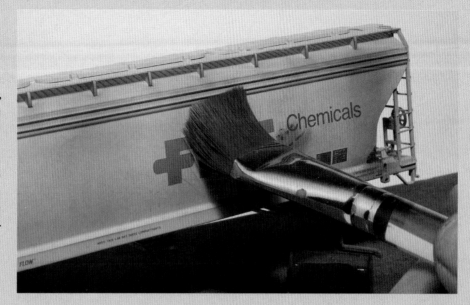

The masking is carefully removed to reveal "freshly painted" patches.

The carbody received a coat of flat varnish to seal the powdered chalks and create a smooth surface for the graffiti decals. Note that none of the powder has disappeared after the varnish.

Applying graffiti and tags

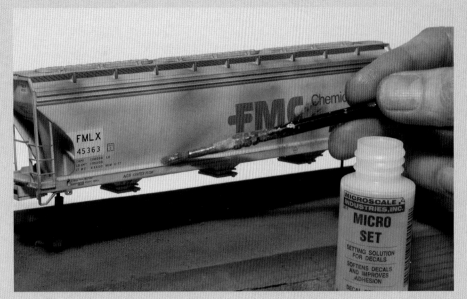

Start by cutting out the decals you want on your car. Trim off as much of the clear decal film as you can so only the printed area remains and dip it in water. Apply decal-setting solution to the area where you want to place the decal on the freight car.

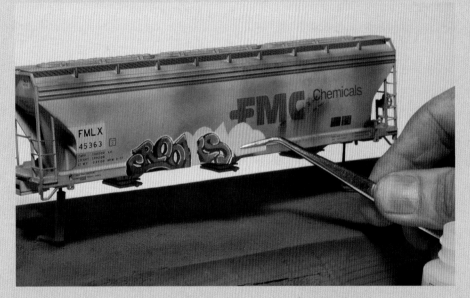

Slide the decal onto the body. My decal broke when I pushed it off the backing paper. This is not uncommon; the fix is to move the two pieces back together when positioning the decal. If it doesn't move easily, just apply more setting solution. When it dries, you'll never know it was torn.

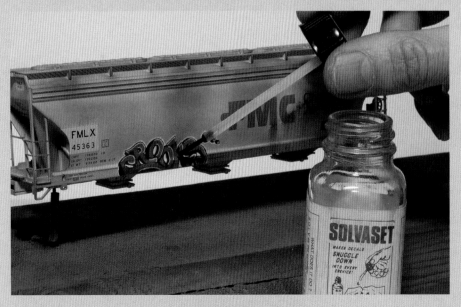

With the decal in its final position, I applied a little Solvaset. Solvaset softens the decal film and makes the decal cling to the surface. It will look as though it had been painted on. When the decals are dry, wipe off traces of setting solution with a damp cloth.

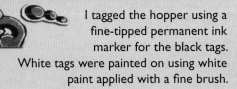

I tagged the hopper using a fine-tipped permanent ink marker for the black tags. White tags were painted on using white paint applied with a fine brush.

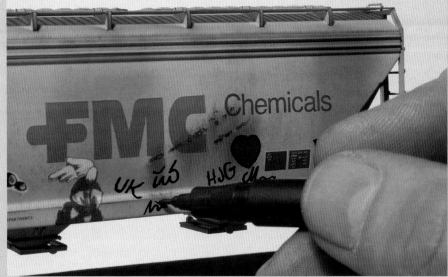

The underside and lower area received a coat of thinned Model Master Dark Skintone. Finally, the entire body received a sealing coat of flat varnish. I used an acrylic varnish from Vallejo, which dries in minutes.

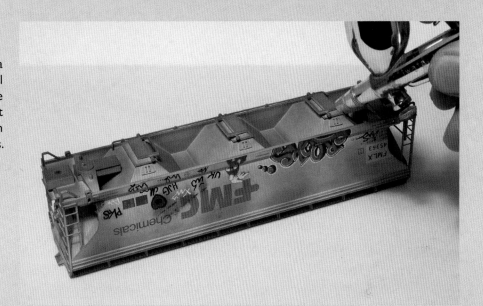

The trucks were airbrushed with a dirty dark gray mix of Model Master Engine Gray and Dark Skintone. To avoid getting paint in the axle bearings, I placed dummy wheelsets in the trucks before painting them.

The wheels need to be painted and weathered too. I paint wheel faces with a gray brown color.

After the paint is dry, the painted wheel face was dabbed with rust-colored powder. To make it easier to spot cracks, real railroad wheels are not painted and will often appear rusty.

the decal film and makes the decal look as though it had been painted on. When the decals are dry, wipe off traces of setting solution with a damp cloth.

I made the tags using a permanent ink marker pen for the black tags and applied white paint with a fine brush for the white tags.

Finally I gave the underside and lower area a coat of thinned Model Master Dark Skintone, and then the entire carbody received a sealing coat of flat varnish.

Aging wheels and trucks

The wheels and trucks need to be weathered too. The trucks were airbrushed with a mix of Model Master Engine Gray and Dark Skintone.

I hand-painted the wheel faces in a brown-gray similar to dark skin tone. When the paint was dry, they were dabbed with rust-colored powder. Assemble the wheels and trucks. Mount the trucks to the body and your vandalized hopper is ready to flash its graffiti all over your layout.

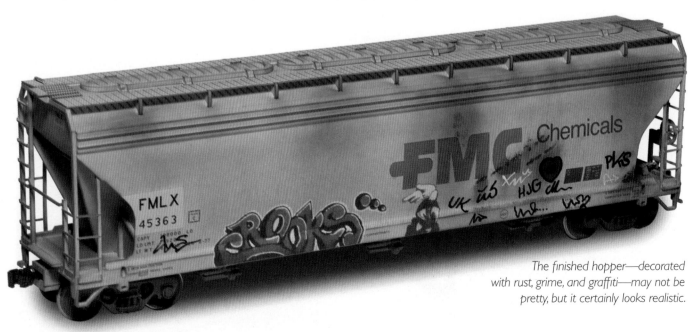

The finished hopper—decorated with rust, grime, and graffiti—may not be pretty, but it certainly looks realistic.

Hopper gallery

This Chicago & North Western covered hopper was weathered using the same techniques described in this chapter. As you can see, the powders are less visible on a dark surface than on a light surface.

Here is another example of a covered hopper with rust spots, grime, and graffiti.

The last example shows a hopper from a fallen-flag railroad. The original road name is almost faded away. Sanding the lettering with very fine sandpaper till it's almost gone does the trick.

Weather a tank car to leave no doubt about what it's carrying

Sometimes you can tell what's inside a tank car just by looking at it. Loading spills around the dome and down the sides give you a pretty good idea of the contents. This Atlas tank car was weathered as an oil tanker by using black paint to simulate spilled oil on the tank.

The basic weathering of the tank described in this chapter can be used on any type of black tank car no matter what contents you are trying to represent. The main difference will be the color of the spilled contents. And remember only a brand new tank car looks totally black. Soon it takes

on a grimy color tone ranging from shades of grays to warmer brownish tones.

The technique for modeling this effect more or less follows that for weathering the hopper and boxcar described in the previous chapters. First the shiny black paint is toned down by a couple of light over-sprays of Model Master Flat Gull Gray. Then powdered chalks do the rest of the basic weathering.

You do not have to worry about applying too much powdered chalk when you are working on a dark surface like on this black tank car. About half of it will dis-

appear when the car receives the sealing coat of clear varnish.

The trucks received my usual mix of Model Master Engine Gray and Dark Skintone. When the paint had dried, they also received some rust-colored powder. And as before, the trucks also received a coat of varnish to seal the powdered chalks.

The wheels were prepared with paint and powdered chalks just as on the previous cars. I also painted the backs of the wheels as well as the axles because they are visible on this type of car.

Now you can apply the type of spill to the tank you prefer. The oil spill on this car is black paint applied with a fine brush.

Weathering freight cars offers a good opportunity to make other small improvements on the models. In this case, it was the ideal time to replace the molded grab irons above the steps with wire ones, since grab irons are prominent on a tank car.

This of course has to be done prior to the weathering. The weathering will completely cover any touch-up.

Here's the Atlas tank car as it appears right out of the box. It does not look much like the filthy tank cars I have seen on my railfan trips.

I replaced the molded grab irons on this car with wire grab irons. To do this, start by trimming off the molded parts.

Then I drilled holes for the new wire grab irons.

I painted the wire grab irons black and patched the traces from the cutting.

The tank body received light coats of Model Master Flat Gull Gray to fade the black and create a flat surface for the powdered chalks.

Apply rust and grime and an oil spill

Powdered chalks used for the tankers are light rust, medium rust, brown, and black. I started by applying light rust to the top of the tank with a soft brush.

I then worked some medium rust into the light rust. Use plenty of powder. Much of it will disappear from the black surface when the tank receives a seal coat of varnish.

Brown and black powders are applied starting from the bottom of the tank and brushed up the sides.

The sealing coat tones down the colors of the powder radically. You can always repeat the procedure with one more layer of powdered chalk if you want the colors to be more intense.

Traces of spilled oil are painted on with a fine brush. I used a black acrylic hobby paint to simulate the oil.

The finished tank car now looks like it's been hard at work. The trucks and wheels have also been weathered.

Weather a tank car so it looks as though it hasn't been weathered at all

Occasionally I like to include a new-looking freight car or two in my train consists. Although it is tempting to simply place a car on the track right out of the box, it never looks quite right. Believe it or not, you need to weather a new straight-from-the-box model to look like a brand-new freight car.

Even within a few miles of the factory, a real freight car will show traces of dust and grime on its surface. And because most of the new body is so fresh and so different than everything else in the consist, a completely untouched car will look even more

unrealistic than an overly weathered car. The trick is to get just the right amount.

I wanted to weather two modern tank cars from Athearn as new cars. My goal was to weather the cars in a way so they appeared as if they haven't been weathered at all. The procedure for this differs a little from more heavily weathered freight cars.

First step is the usual toning down of the car body. However, in this case, I used a darker color than for more heavily weathered freight cars and I applied fewer coats too. Using powdered chalks was limited to

the area around the domes. Just like the other freight cars in this book, the tankers received some road grime along the lower area and underside but only a single light coat.

The cars will now appear more dusty and grimy than a new car would but on a dark surface most of the dusty look will disappear when the tankers receive their final coat of varnish.

To get rid of the shiny plastic look of the trucks, they have to be painted. I airbrushed them with a grayish black called Tire Black from Vallejo. A distinct feature

The top photo shows the Athearn tanker as it appears right out of the box. On the photo below, you can see the tanker as it appears after it has received a discrete weathering. The tank is not as deep black anymore and a little less glossy. A more realistic-looking grimy flat black replaces the plastic shine on the trucks, and the wheels are rust colored rather than grimy and oily as they would be on older cars.

on new freight cars is the blue roller bearing end caps on the trucks. On older trucks, the blue is covered with rust and grime. Details like painting the roller bearing end caps light blue helps to re-create the appearance of a new freight car.

The initial impression is a car with no weathering. Only if you place it next to a car straight from the box you will notice a difference between the two cars.

On the pictures above you can compare the tanker that has been weatherized with one straight from the box. The new tanker below still appears new but in a more realistic way than the one on top.

A handy tool for removing dust is an old dust-removing brush for working with photographic film. When the bulb is squeezed, air from between the bristles blows away the dust loosened by the soft brush.

Apply a discrete weathering

The first step is the usual toning down of the carbody's deep black. Instead of using a light gray or sand color for this, I chose a dark gray. I thinned Model Master Dark Sea Gray to a wash and applied it in two light coats.

The lower area and underside received a light coat of thinned Model Master Dark Skintone. If you think your car looks a little too dusty and grimy, don't worry. It will change when it receives a sealing coat of varnish later.

The difference between this type of weathering and the others described in this book is that I used almost no powdered chalks on this model. Only the area around the domes received a little brown and black powdered chalk.

The tank car is supposed to look new so instead of giving the car body a coat of flat varnish I gave it a sealing coat of Vallejo Satin Varnish instead. The varnish absorbs some of the gray and brown I sprayed on earlier so it appear less noticeable.

To avoid getting paint in the axle bearings I replaced the wheels with dummy wheelsets. The trucks were painted in a weathered black color, in this case Vallejo Tire Black.

I painted the roller bearing end caps light blue, which seems to be the norm on new freight car trucks. After that the trucks also received a light coat of thinned Model Master Dark Skintone. The wheels were first painted with Dark Skintone and then dabbed with medium rust, which looks like the fresh rust seen on new wheels.

The trucks received a final coat of flat varnish. I snapped the wheelsets back in the trucks and painted the axles and wheel backs with Dark Skin Tone. It's ready to be reinstalled on the car.

A rusted roof is the key to a realistically weathered old auto carrier

During my railfan trips, I have noticed that the roofs of older enclosed auto carriers seem to have severe rust problems, and I thought it would be fun to replicate the look for my layout.

I have several of these cars, but I am particularly fond of one of them, my Union Pacific bi-level auto carrier, which dates back to my previous layout. It started as an undecorated Walthers model. I have replaced the molded ladder steps with brass wire and have added a brake chain and rod details to it. The molded stirrup steps have been cut off and replaced with new

ones made from flat brass bar. I painted and lettered the car too.

The car has served me well for many years and deserved to represent a different era on my present layout. It was already weathered, but I wanted to give the car a second and much-heavier weathering treatment.

It definitely called for a rusted roof, but I didn't want to take it as far as some I have seen where the entire roof was solid rust. I aimed for a more-moderate rusted roof on my UP auto carrier with rust attacks on about half of the roof panels.

I used a slightly different technique for applying rust on the roof than the usual application of powdered chalks on wet varnish. This time, I pre-mixed varnish with some rust colored powdered chalks (see page 42). I applied the mix with a brush to one or two small areas at a time. While the coat is still wet, I apply more rust powder to the area.

After rust had been applied randomly to the entire roof, I brushed the excess rust powder down the sides of the body. This simulates how the rust has been washed down the sides by rain.

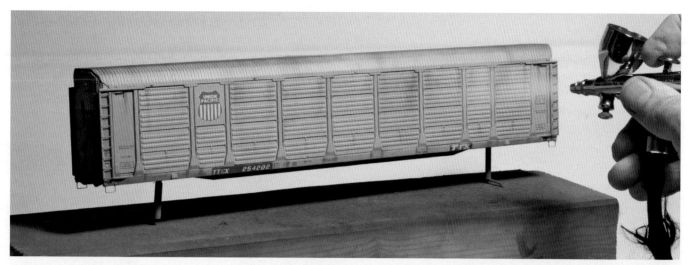

As usual, I started by toning down the original Athearn carrier's paint with a gray beige, thinned to a wash and applied with an airbrush.

I have seen auto carriers with rust streaks like these running down the sides but also having a sparkling clean roof. The rusted roof that caused the streaks had apparently been replaced with a new roof. This is one case where it's probably best to leave well enough alone. It would look too weird to put a new roof on such a rusted body even though you can find a prototype for it.

The rest of the weathering process followed my general practice with the combination of powdered chalks and thinned paint applied with an airbrush.

A Blair Line graffiti decal was applied to the car. After the decal was softened with Solvaset, I gently tapped the decal with the tip of the brush to make it conform to the car's irregular surface.

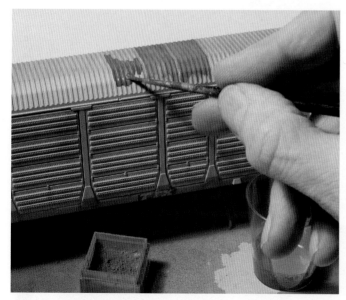

I mixed some rust powder with clear varnish and painted some of the roof panels with the mix.

While the powder/varnish mix was still wet, I applied more rust powder to the area with a soft brush.

Smudging the car body

I brushed excess rust powder from the roof with downward strokes. This simulates how the rust has been washed down the car's sides by rain.

The dominant weathering powder on this car is rust, but some brown and black powders are also applied to the sides and to the roof.

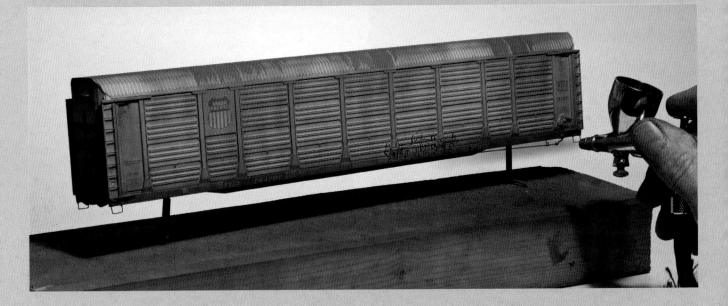

The underside and lower area received the usual coat of thinned Model Master Dark Skintone, and after that, the entire body received a sealing coat of flat varnish.

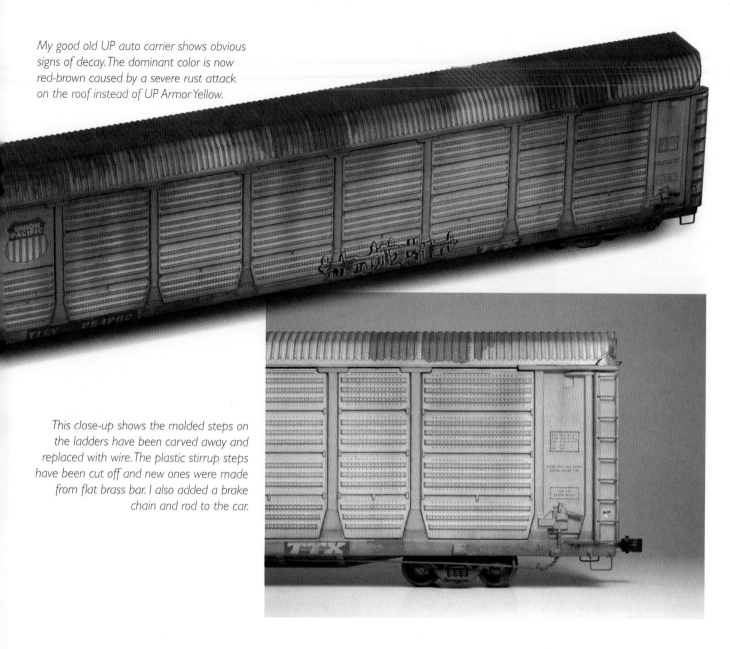

My good old UP auto carrier shows obvious signs of decay. The dominant color is now red-brown caused by a severe rust attack on the roof instead of UP Armor Yellow.

This close-up shows the molded steps on the ladders have been carved away and replaced with wire. The plastic stirrup steps have been cut off and new ones were made from flat brass bar. I also added a brake chain and rod to the car.

Here's another auto carrier that received a treatment similar to the one described on these pages, except for the modifications of the ladders and steps.

Give your first-generation double-stack cars a contemporary look

I was preparing to make a new stack train for my layout to represent a coast-to-coast train hauling nothing but 20-, 40- and 45-foot containers.

Athearn had just introduced a very nice version of the Gunderson Maxi I 5-unit well car. These early cars were meant for 40-foot containers and therefore shorter than later well cars, which can haul containers up to the 53' long.

Short cars have an advantage if you have limited layout space, as I do. This allows you to run more cars on a maximum-length train. Fortunately you still see these older well cars around, giving me an excuse to use them for a stack train on my layout even though it is represents a contemporary line.

Of course these first-generation well cars do not look new any more. In fact

they appear pretty ratty with rust and grime everywhere, so there was no way out except to give my new stack cars a full weathering treatment.

Such treatment includes fading the cars' original paint, applying rust spots and scratches, and adding a general layer of grime to the five wells. I have noticed that the ends of these cars especially appear very dirty.

Preparing and weathering the well cars

I removed the trucks from the car. I also removed the yellow span bolsters from the shared trucks as I airbrushed all the trucks with grimy black.

Before starting the weathering, I gently wiped the well sides with a damp cloth to remove any fingerprint grease. I discovered that several of the metal walkways had loosened, and I secured them with a dab of cyanoacrylate adhesive (CA) before I started weathering the cars.

All units in an articulated car will normally appear equally weathered so it was important that all five wells receive the same amount of paint and powdered chalks so none of them would stand out.

The best way to ensure even treatment is to set up a production line and finish each step of the weathering procedure on all the units before proceeding with the next step.

Containers need weathering too

Also, the containers needed to be weathered in order to appear realistic.

If you have watched a stack train pass, you have probably noticed that some containers look brand new while others are faded and/or dirty. Some have rust spots here and there. Again some are patched with new paint.

Unlike each well of the five-unit car, I gave the containers various degrees of weathering because I wanted my stack train to contain a mix of older and newer containers just as you see them on real stack trains.

I removed the floor from each container and placed the bodies on blocks cut from foam insulation board. I had trimmed these blocks for a tight fit to prevent the container bodies from falling off while I worked on them. The floors were taped to a stick.

The containers were weathered the same way as I weather my freight cars in general.

A photo of my nice, new Athearn well car loaded with spotless containers. This is going to change soon.

Setting up the production line

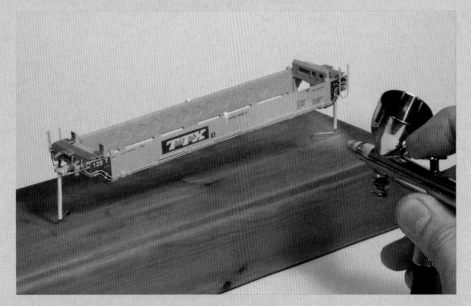

The Maxi 1 well car consists of five units, each of which has to be weathered individually. First, all five-unit wells received the usual coat of thinned Model Master Sand. Remember to give the inside walls a coat too. This bleaches the car's original colors and leaves a nice flat surface, perfect for weathering.

I mixed a rust paste from rust-colored powdered chalks and Vallejo Flat varnish. You can use rust-colored paint instead, but I prefer the powder/varnish mix because it leaves a slightly textured surface, which looks very much like real rust.

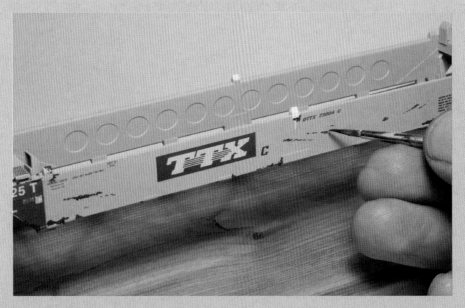

To create rust spots and scratches, I dabbed the rust paste on the well sides with a fine brush. Rust can typically be found where there is wear and tear, especially around welding seams and along edges. I dabbed all five units with rust paste before I proceeded with the next steps.

I applied dry rust-colored powdered chalks on the rust spots and dragged the brush down to create the look of streaks of rust washed down the sides by rain.

Then I applied black and brown powdered chalks to the well sides with a wide soft brush. Do not forget to give the inside walls their share too in case you want to run the cars empty.

The lower areas and ends on all five units received a light coat of thinned Model Master Dark Skintone. Finally all five wells received a sealing coat of flat varnish.

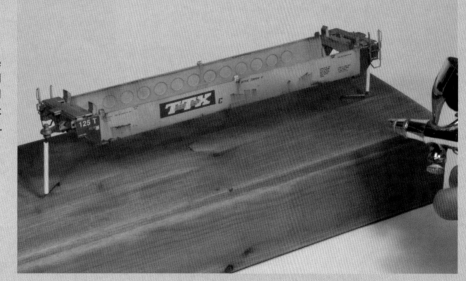

I masked all bearings for the axles with a liquid masking product from Humbrol called Maskol. I then sprayed the trucks a grimy black color. When they were dry, I applied some rust powder randomly to the truck sideframes. Finally everything was sealed with a flat varnish. The wheels were weathered as described on page 26.

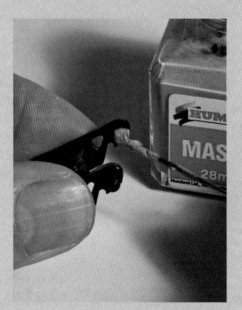

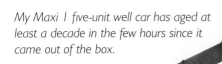

My Maxi 1 five-unit well car has aged at least a decade in the few hours since it came out of the box.

Rust will typically be present where there is wear and tear such as on the container guides.

The end platform's many details stand out more prominently after the weathering.

The close-up shows weathering on the truck and wheels. Also note how the rust spots and dirt on the well sides make the car look old.

The loading and unloading of countless containers have damaged the paint on the reservoir shield, which has caused it to rust.

The containers were weathered the same way as the well car. They too had their original paint faded with light over-sprays of gray beige and then were dabbed with pre-mixed rust paste and dry rust-colored powder.

The ends of the finished containers show that each didn't receive the same amount of weathering.

The entire container body received rust, brown, and black powdered chalks applied with a wide soft brush. Like my freight cars, everything was sealed with Vallejo Flat Finish. You can also see the block cut from foam insulation board I use for handling the container while I am working on it.

An easy flatcar pipe load made from Evergreen styrene tubing

No railroad makes money running empty freight cars, and my HO layout is no exception. Although you can buy ready-made freight car loads, most loads are not hard to make, and by doing so, you can model exactly what you have seen on your railfan excursions.

For example, during my field trips, I started paying careful attention to loads of pipe and other long bulky materials and how different types of loads are stacked and secured.

Since I had several open freight cars on my layout that needed some kind of loads, and since stacked pipes seem to be

a common load on flatcars, I decided to make such a load for one of my Walthers bulkhead flats.

I started by cutting in equal lengths some Evergreen ⁹⁄₃₂" styrene tubes I had in stock. For this load, I needed a total of 15 pipes. With smaller diameter tubes you need more.

The most common colors I've seen for pipe are black or red. I chose red for my pipe load and airbrushed the Evergreen tubes with a reddish color mixed from Model Master Gloss Ferrari Red having just a touch of flat white and Burnt Umber added to it. A mix of gloss and flat paint

leaves a silky finish when dry. The pipes in the prototype pipe loads I have seen have all been glossy, but in scale, I believe a semi-gloss finish looks more realistic.

The inside and ends of the pipes are supposed to be gray. My hand is not steady enough to do this freehand, so I wrapped a piece of masking tape around the ends ¹⁄₆₄" from the edge and painted the ends and the inside of the pipes gray.

Stacking the pipes

Wood strips are placed between the layers of pipes on a flatcar to prevent the

I cut a total of 15 pipes in equal lengths from Evergreen 9/32" styrene tube.

The tubes were painted red. I wrapped them with strips of masking tape close to the ends.

The ends and insides of the tubes were painted gray.

pipes from rolling over the edge. The first layers of pipe are placed on six wood strips with small blocks attached to the ends to keep the pipes in place. The wood strips are spaced evenly. I drew a template on a sheet of paper as a guideline.

Wood strips go between all layers except the top one. The layers have equal amounts of pipe except the top layer, which consists of one less pipe. This way the top layer can rest in the grooves between the pipes in the layer below.

The first two layers are first wrapped together with straps separately and then all layers are banded with straps.

The pipes are ready to stack. Having the ends and insides painted a contrasting color gives an extra realistic appearance.

Mounting the load to the flatcar deck

My pipe load appears to be attached to the flatcar with elastic strings. Actually I glued it to the flatcar deck first, but a real load would be attached to the car by straps pulled over the load and fastened to the car's side sills.

I use the heavy version of a product called EZ Line—an elastic string from Berkshire Junction—for these straps.

Apply a dab of super glue in four of the side sill pockets and stick the end of a piece of EZ Line in each of them. Pull the EZ Line over the load and attach it with a

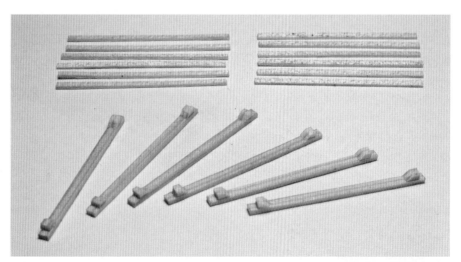

Six pieces of stripwood are needed for this load. The strips with the wood blocks attached are for the flatcar deck and carry the weight of the entire load, which is why it is made from heavier wood than the other strips.

Stacking the pipes

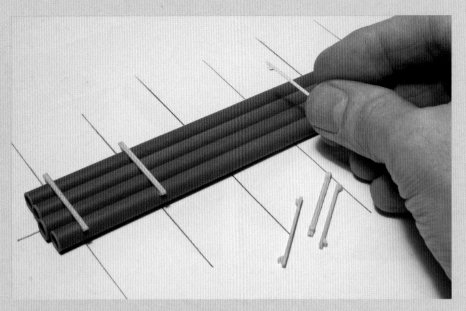

I sketched guidelines on a sheet of paper and placed the first layer of pipes on it. The pre-made strips of wood with little blocks attached to the ends are glued to the pipes with super glue—six in total.

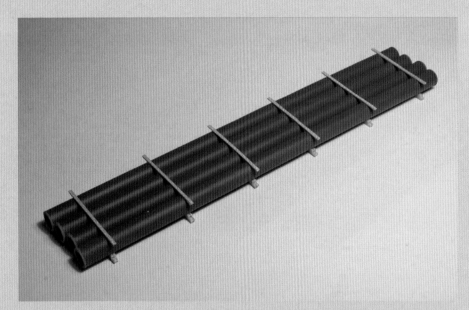

Turn the section of pipes over and glue another set of stripwood braces to the pipes directly above the first layer of wood strips.

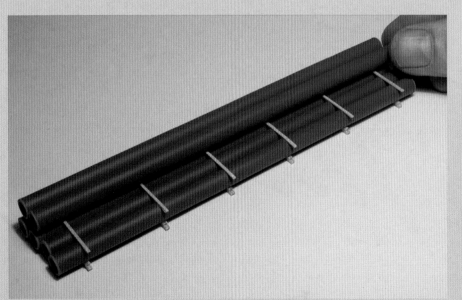

Apply the next layer of pipes. Glue them to the wood strips with super glue. There is no need to align the ends of pipes; let some of them stick out a little more than the others. In the real world, the guys loading freight cars don't bother if everything is neatly aligned.

Turn the load around so the bottom is facing up. Now wrap the two sections with thin strips of black tape. The tape was secured with a dab of super glue. I cut the tape strips from black insulation tape.

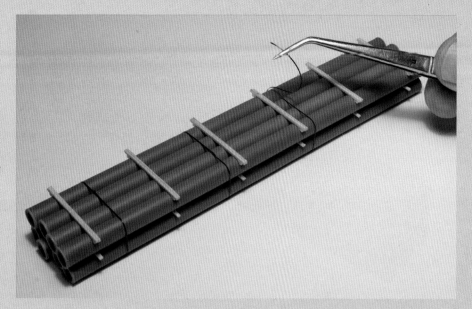

Turn the load over again and apply a new layer of stripwood to it.

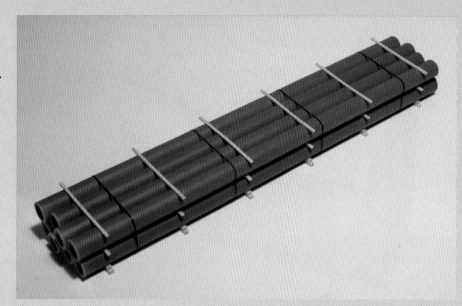

Apply another layer of pipes the same way as before. Make sure that the stack is vertical.

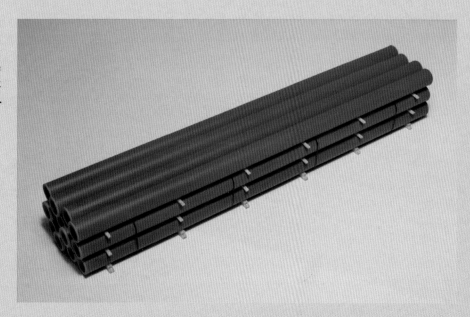

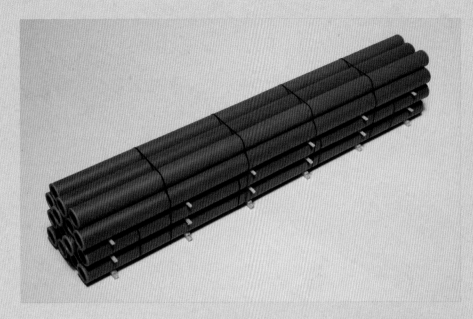

Apply the last layer of pipes. There is no need for stripwood between the last two layers as the pipes on the top rest in the grooves between the pipes below. Everything was secured with super glue.

Wrap the load with strips of the black tape and secure each wrap with a dab of glue as before.

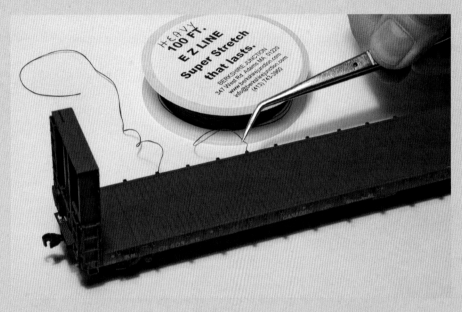

Wires to hold the load on the flat car were made from EZ Line—an elastic string. I used the heavy version for this. Apply a dab of super glue in four of the side sill pockets and stick the end of a piece of EZ Line in each of them.

Place the load on the car, securing it with a little super glue. Pull the EZ Line over the load and attach it with a dab of glue in the side sill pocket on this side of the car. That's it—the car is ready to roll with its new load.

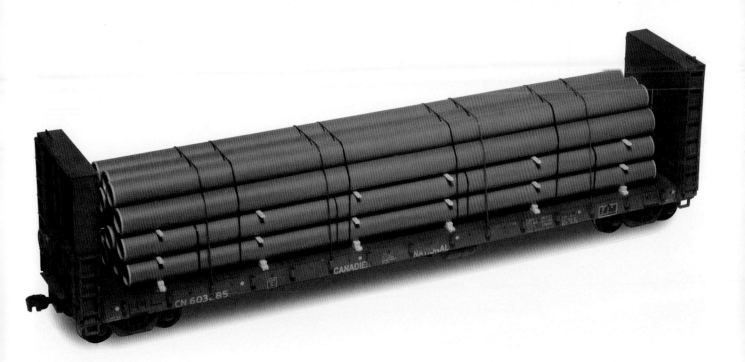

dab of glue in the opposite side sill pocket of the flatcar.

Above you can see the finished load mounted on the car. You can use the same method for making other types of loads for your bulkhead flatcars. Below you can see examples of two other loads I have made: concrete beams and steel H-beams.

The concrete load was made from rectangular styrene tubes. The ends were closed with pieces of styrene, and the beams were painted in a concrete color mixed from equal parts of Model Master flat Gull Gray, Sand, and White. The beams were wrapped with strips of black tape just like the pipe load and placed on wood strips.

The other load was made from Evergreen H-beams. The load consists only of two layers as it represents a heavier load than the pipes.

The Evergreen H-beams were cut in equal lengths and painted in a reddish primer color. Then they were stacked with stripwood between the layers and wrapped with black tape like the other loads.

Both loads were also attached to the flatcar with elastic strings the same way as the pipe load.

Loading a gondola with stainless steel pipes made from aluminum tubes

You can find all kinds of loads in gondolas. I spotted this stainless steel pipe load on one of my recent railfan trips (see photo on page 13), and I had to have one rolling on my HO layout.

I had a hard time finding the right tubes for such a load, but at last I found them in a hobby shop specializing in model airplanes. They had all kinds of light-weight building materials and amongst them were 3mm (⅛") aluminum tubing. Not only were they the perfect size, they could also be used as they were. The aluminum looked pretty much like stainless steel and no painting was necessary.

Cutting the tubes

The tubes came in one meter (3.3-foot) lengths. I needed a total of 60 pipes, each 34 scale feet long.

Aluminum is soft, and I found that the easiest way to cut the tubes was with a very sharp knife. I placed the blade on the tube with a moderate pressure and rolled the tube back and forth till it separated.

I sanded the ends of the tubes by holding them lightly against a rotating cutting disk. To make the pipes look more realistic I widened the holes in the ends with a high-speed cutter.

Assembling the load

The pipes are not just tossed in the gondola but stacked carefully and supported by wood and straps. I made two wood braces as support for the pipes from pieces of stripwood. Each brace consisted of two horizontal beams and six vertical posts—three on each side.

I stacked the pipes between the posts and glued down eight pipes, which formed the first layer, to the horizontal beams on which the entire load will be resting.

I then placed seven pipes on the first layer. Then, I put eight pipes on top of the seven and so forth until I reached a total of eight layers. Each layer was glued to the pipes below.

Both ends of the pipe stack were wrapped with three thin strips of black tape. I secured the tape below the load with super glue.

The load was fastened with six straps glued to the vertical wood posts. For the straps, I used the heavy version of EZ Line, which was glued to the posts with super glue.

I placed the load in one of my Athearn gondolas. However, I did not glue it to the freight car as it seemed heavy enough not to shift, without being glued. A couple of test runs put my mind at ease about it.

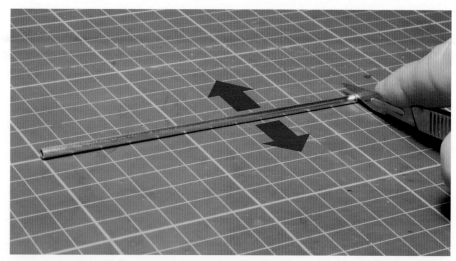

The aluminum tube can be cut with a sharp knife. Press the knife blade against the tube and roll it back and forth till it separates.

The ends of the pipes are sanded smooth by holding them lightly against a rotating disk cutter.

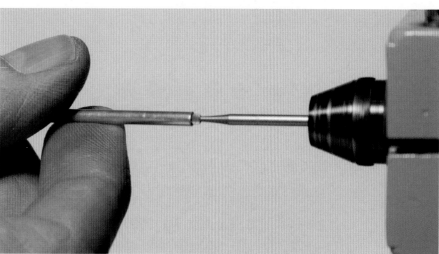

Widening the pipe openings with a high-speed cutter thins the material and gives the pipes a more realistic appearance.

Assembling the pipe load

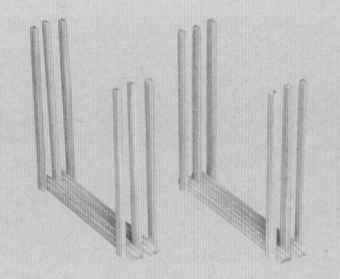

I made two wood braces for pipe supports. Each of them consisted of two horizontal beams with six vertical posts—three at each side—mounted to them. The vertical beams are a little lighter than the horizontal beams. I glued the pieces together with ordinary white carpenter's glue.

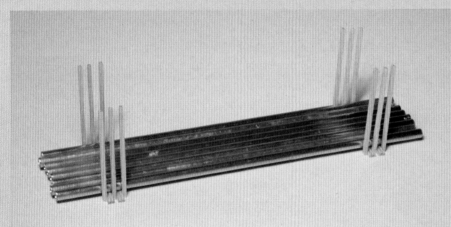

The first layer of pipes was placed in the braces and glued to the horizontal beams with super glue.

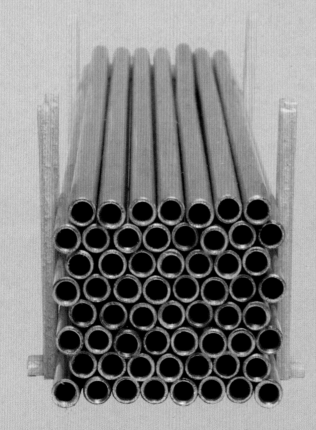

The stack consists of eight layers alternating between eight and seven pipes per layer. That way, each layer is placed so the pipes rest in the grooves between the pipes below. The pipes were held together with super glue.

Both ends of the pipes were wrapped with thin strips of black tape. I cut the tape strips from black insulation tape. The tape ends were secured with a dab of super glue at the underside of the load.

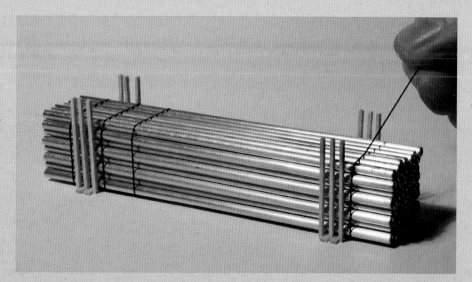

I secured the load with six straps. The straps are mounted to the vertical wood beams on one side and pulled across the load and mounted to the beams at the opposite side. For this I used the heavy version of EZ Line. The string was glued to the posts with super glue.

All that remained to be done was to place the load in the Athearn gondola, and it was ready to roll.

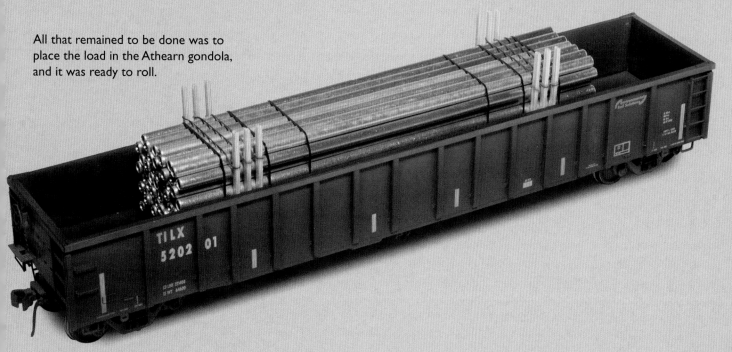

Make a heavy steel coil load for your gondolas from styrene strips

Loads of coiled steel are a common sight in gondolas, and I had a couple of gons just begging for such a load.

Some time ago, I had bought a steel coil freight car load from Chooch Enterprises. However, the coils turned out to be intended as flatcar loads where the coils are placed on their sides and so they lacked detail on both sides of the coil.

In a gondola, the rolls are placed vertically, the same way as they are placed in coil cars. I decided to make my own coils rather than place them in an unprotoypical position. I figured that the easiest way to make the coils would be using thin styrene strips wound to a coil. I started with cutting ½-inch-wide strips from a .010" styrene sheet.

The strips were 12 inches long, which was determined by the size of the styrene sheet. Each coil consisted of three strips, so in total, each coil contained 36 inches of strip styrene.

I wound the strip styrene as tight as I could around an Evergreen styrene tube, and secured the ends with glue.

The coils received a coat of Model-Master "Steel" metallic paint applied with an airbrush. Model Master "Steel" leaves a grayish metal look. If you want the ap-pearance of a shiny metal, Model Master "Chrome Silver" is an option.

Finally each coil was wrapped with thin strips of black tape to simulate the metal bands holding the coil together.

Winding the coils

I started with cutting a quantity of ½"-wide strips from .010" styrene sheet. Each strip is 12" long, and to complete one coil you'll need three strips.

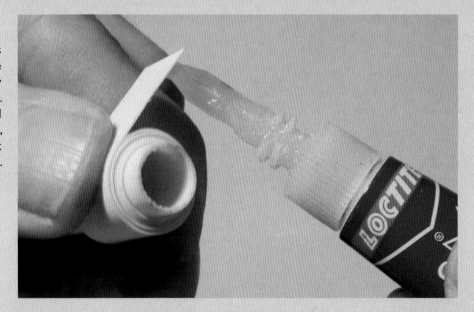

The first layer of styrene strip was wound around a ⅜" Evergreen styrene tube, but you can use a pen or any other round object for the purpose. Wind the strip as tightly as possible and secure the end with glue. I used CA, which bonded instantly. Be careful that the strip stays tight around the tube.

Now glue the next strip to the end of the first. Wind a second tight layer and secure it with glue just like the first layer. Repeat the procedure with a third layer.

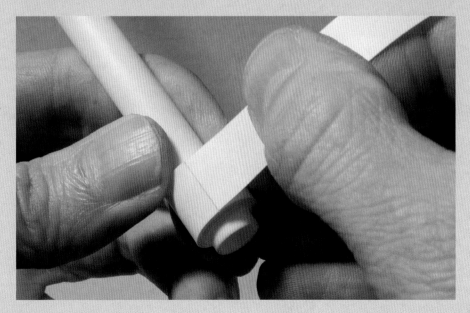

Finishing the coils

I airbrushed the coils with a coat of Model Master No. 1780 Steel. I placed the coil on the tip of a pen and painted one side, then turned it upside down and sprayed the other. Just applying the metal paint seemed to make them look heavy.

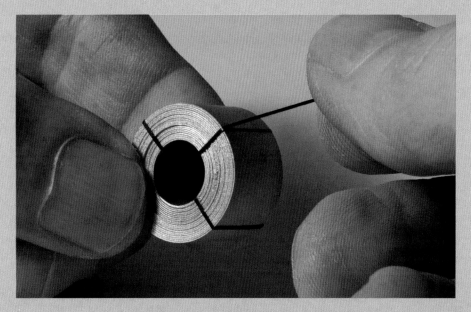

I cut strips from black electical tape and wrapped four thin strips on each coil.

Here's a finished set of coils ready to be loaded in a gondola. I was quite pleased with their appearance, which made it worth the effort of making my own coils.

The coils are not just tossed in a gondola but placed in a wooden or metal crate to support them during transportation.

I made a wooden crate for one of the loads out of stripwood. The second load was placed in a metal crate that came with a Walthers gondola.

The coils are normally placed as pairs in each end of a gondola right above the trucks. The coils are very heavy, and often a full load consists of only four coils.

The wooden crate has a simple design: just five pieces of stripwood glued together. I glued the coils to the crates.

I made the wood crates wide enough so that they could be secured by pressing them in place. That way I could avoid gluing them to the gondola floor in case I later wanted to load my gondola with something else.

Easy-to-make removable loads for your open hoppers

One of the easiest freight car loads to make is a load for an open hopper. And the most common type of loose-material load is probably coal. Others are ballast or rock, also easy to model.

It seems most hopper models come with plastic loads nowadays, so why bother to make your own? The problem is that the loads just didn't look realistic enough for my taste. Plastic will always look like plastic.

One thing to watch for is that the load is removable. This is handy if you also want to run the hopper empty.

The easiest way to make a better-looking coal load is to simply apply a new load on top of the plastic load. That way you still have a removable load, but one that's better looking than the plastic version.

This one took less than five minutes to complete, which you'll appreciate if you need to model an entire coal train consist. All you need for the job is a bag of model coal and some white glue. Various manufacturers of scenery products offer coal in different sizes.

I used Woodland Scenics Mine Run Coal for this Athearn hopper load. I brushed the top of the plastic load with a

layer of slow-drying glue, and then sprinkled coal on the wet glue until the surface was completely covered. After a couple of hours when the glue had dried, I shook all loose material off the load and placed it back in the hopper.

I make loads for my ballast hoppers the exact same way. Instead of gluing coal, I just use some ballast left over from when I ballasted my track.

Making a coal load

I removed the hopper's plastic load and brushed a layer of white carpenter's glue on the top surface, being careful not to get any glue on the sides.

Then I poured a layer of Woodland Scenics coal on the wet glue. I gently pressed the coal into the glue with the tip of my finger. After the glue had dried, I held the load in a vertical position while I tapped it a couple of times on the back side to knock off any loose material.

What could be simpler? This Athearn hopper looks so much better than it would with a plastic load.

How to give your once-beautiful Warbonnets a hard-at-work, weathered look

My all-time favorite locomotive paint scheme is Santa Fe's red and silver "warbonnet" livery. When American trains caught my interest in the early '90s, Santa Fe had just re-introduced the warbonnet paint scheme, and I was sold the minute I saw a lash-up of these sparkling new red and silver diesels passing by.

We all know what happened since the merger with Burlington Northern and the introduction of the green and orange paint schemes. You may still be lucky enough to see a diesel or two in classic Warbonnet colors, but their condition is likely to be

a depressing sight. The only good thing I can say about the situation is that it has created a challenge for modelers who like weathering locomotives.

Common details to watch for are replacement parts like an air conditioner or metal panels. These parts will not only appear cleaner but may even be in a different color than the original part.

The paint is often in a bad shape. The red will be faded with bleached spots scattered all over. I don't know what causes these spots but I have seen it on several old Warbonnets. Rust is, of course, present all over the locomotive. The roof will be filthy black from soot and grime. The trucks, fuel tank, and other lower areas will be covered with road grime.

Getting started

I decided to ruin the good looks of a beautiful red and silver Atlas Dash 8-40CW by giving it a weathered, working warbonnet look. The process involved more steps than my usual weathering, and to be honest, it probably can't be done on a single Sunday afternoon. You may need to start this one

Here's a pretty Atlas Dash 8-40CW as it looks right out of the box: That's about to change.

on a Saturday if you want a weathered locomotive like this ready to run on your layout by the end of the weekend.

First, I separated the shell from the frame. I also removed the side handrails to be able to apply masking tape around the air conditioner and a panel, which had to be painted to look like a replaced part. The trucks were separated from the frame, and the sideframes and wheels were separated from them.

The first step was masking the areas that should be repainted. I wanted to paint the air conditioner orange to make it look as if it has been replaced with one from a newer BNSF locomotive. A panel on the right side of the shell is painted silver to make it look as if it has been newly replaced.

A couple of small details needed to be painted too. The headlight was painted silver and so were the antennas on the cab roof. The tips of the m.u. hoses were also painted silver.

With these preparations, the model is ready for the actual weathering process.

The area around one of the panels on the right side of the shell was covered with masking tape. The panel will be painted silver to make it look as if it has been newly replaced. The air conditioner seen in the picture below will be painted orange.

First step: Painting

A panel on the on the right side of the shell and the air conditioner on the left side both had to be painted to make them look as if they had been replaced with newer parts. I masked the area around the parts with masking tape and paper. The panel received a coat of silver paint.

Orange doesn't cover very well, and you need a neutral color on which to apply it, so I also gave the air conditioner a coat of silver as primer before I sprayed it with BNSF orange.

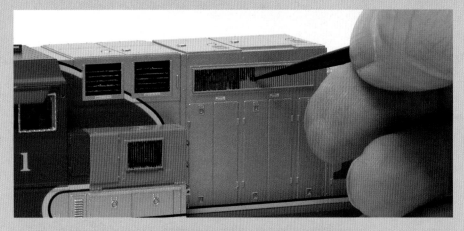

All grilles and air intakes except the big radiator top grille received a black wash to make them stand out. I used black Vallejo Air right out of the bottle for this. Paints in the Vallejo Air series are so thin they look like a wash compared to other brands.

When the black paint was dry, I scraped the top of the grilles with a scalpel. Be careful not the scrape off any of the locomotive's colors.

To prepare the shell for airbrushing, I cut small pieces of masking tape in shapes to fit windows and number boards. It can be a bit tricky to place the masking tape on windows with windshield wipers. I carefully bent the wiper outwards with the tip of a knife and slid the tape under it. Main headlights and ditch lights received a dab of liquid mask.

The bleached spots were painted on the red area with a fine brush. Don't forget the red lettering on both sides of the engine compartment. The color I used was a light gray with a drop of red added. Don't be scared if you think the spots look too drastic. When the overall bleaching and the weathering powders are applied later, the spots will blend perfectly with the rest.

The newly painted air conditioner and panel were covered with masking tape before airbrushing and the handrails were re-installed. I then wiped the shell clean from finger grease with a dry piece of cloth.

Bleaching, rust, and grime

The shell, frame, and truck side-frames received an overall coat of Model Master Light Ghost Gray to give the original paint a sun-bleached look. The gray was thinned to a wash-like consistency, and the parts received two coats each. The roof and walkways received an extra coat to make them appear lighter than the rest.

I removed the masking on the repainted air conditioner and side panel after the fading process.

To create rust spots and scratches, I dabbed the shell with rust paste made from rust-colored powdered chalks and clear varnish (see page 42). I then applied dry rust-colored powdered chalks on the rust spots and dragged the brush downward to create the look of rust streaks washed down the sides by rain. Rust will typically be present where there is wear and tear, around welding seams and along edges.

I worked some black powder in the big radiator grille to add some depth to it. You can give it a wash like the rest of the grilles if you prefer, but this grille has a different shape than the rest, and I think you get a more-realistic result with powdered chalks.

The area around the exhaust and the rest of the roof also received black powdered chalks. The entire roof was covered, but the areas around the exhaust received most with less being applied toward the ends.

To simulate grime and dirt, the sides of the engine compartment and both ends of the cab were also brushed with powdered chalks. For that I used black and brown.

The fuel tank and air tanks received the same treatment as the rest of the locomotive with rust and vertical streaks of grime and dirt. The frame and tank has already been sprayed with Light Ghost Gray, which makes a fine base for applying powders.

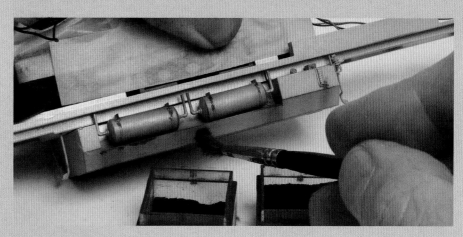

Like the fuel tank, the truck sideframes have been flattened with Light Ghost Gray, and of course, they also need rust and grime to match the rest of the locomotive.

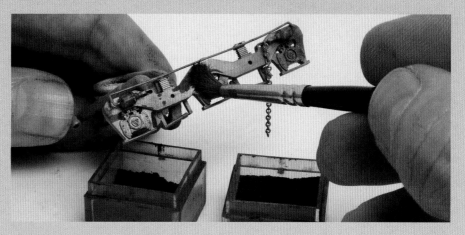

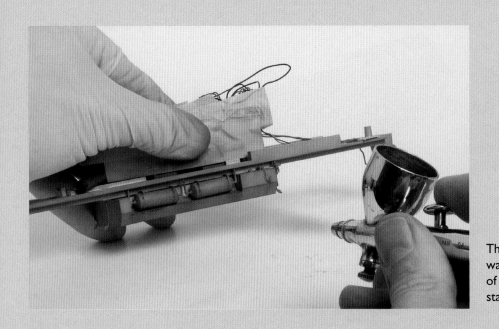

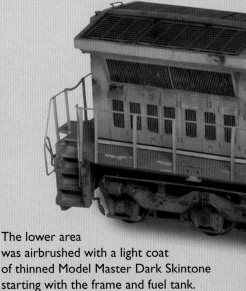

The lower area was airbrushed with a light coat of thinned Model Master Dark Skintone starting with the frame and fuel tank.

The shell also received a light coat of thinned Model Master Dark Skintone along the lower area. The front and rear pilots received a little heavier coat than the sides. Don't forget to give the truck sideframes their share too.

Finally everything was sealed with a coat of Vallejo Satin Varnish.

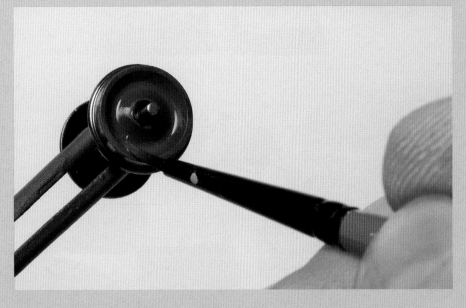

Only one thing remains to be weathered—the wheels. I painted the wheel faces with Model Master Dark Skintone. Be careful not to paint the knob in the center of the wheel, as it is used for electrical pickup and even the slightest amount of paint will cause problems.

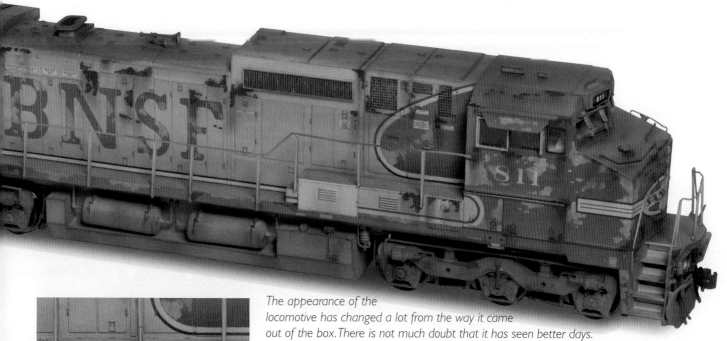

The appearance of the locomotive has changed a lot from the way it came out of the box. There is not much doubt that it has seen better days.

A panel with no stripes that looks cleaner than the rest indicates that it has been replaced recently.

The orange air conditioner is a distinct detail that tells a story.

Peeling lettering and rusted doors on the engine compartment tell us that maintenance hasn't had the highest priority on this locomotive.

From a front view, it's easy to imagine the locomotive in its once-stunning appearance.

A few improvements and a light weathering bring this Atlas Dash 8-40CW up to date

Today's locomotive models are so well detailed that you more or less can run them right out of the box. However, to make a locomotive appear more realistic, you have to at least give it some weathering. On this Atlas Dash 8-40CW, I'll demonstrate the process all locomotives have to go through before they are placed in service on my layout.

This particular model of the first generation of "wide cabs" came in UP's lightning-stripe-and-wing logo, which indicates that it has been newly repainted and required only a light weathering.

A few things have to be done before the actual weathering. First of all, I do not like the illuminated number boards on these Atlas models. The number boards and headlights are cast together in clear plastic, so I separated the number boards from the headlight section. The blanked number boards at the rear end were also separated from the light section. Even though the blanked number boards are painted yellow, the light will shine through the yellow paint if you do not separate them.

I gave the area around the head and rear lights a thick coat of black paint in-

side the shell to completely block any light from showing through the yellow paint.

The Atlas Dash 8-40CW came with a window in the nose door, which would not be not prototypically correct on this locomotive. UP has blanked the window in the nose door on older GEs. This would probably have been done when the locomotives were in for a major overhaul, so this repainted locomotive definitely should have a blanked nose window.

To do this, I started by carefully cutting off the lip around the window. Then I trimmed a piece of styrene to fit the window opening and glued it in place flush with the door. Be very careful not to damage the paint on the door.

I also noted that the headlight on the model is yellow and not silver. I checked prototype photos, and the lights turned out to be yellow, so I would guess the headlights had not been masked when the locomotive was repainted.

I mixed yellow to match the locomotives from Humbrol 154 with a tiny bit of 70 added to it. You can still tell where the window was, and that looks right, as the UP welded a metal plate in the opening,, and it's visible on their locomotives too.

I then added a Details West GPS dome (No. 235-320) to the cab roof, which I have seen on a few of UP's Dash 8-40CWs.

Preparing the model for weathering

You don't have to dismantle the model before you apply the weathering. I only separated the shell from the frame and removed the wheels on this one.

The major difference between weathering freight cars and locomotives is that locomotives have windows and headlights that need to be masked before you start the airbrushing.

The Atlas Dash 8-40CW as it looks right out of the box. Even though it represents a newly repainted locomotive it will appear more realistic with a light weathering.

The number boards and headlights are cast together in clear plastic. I don't like illuminated number boards and separated them from the headlight section with a rotating steel cutter.

The blanked number boards on the rear were also separated from the light section.

To prevent any light from shining through the plastic shell, I coated the inside with a layer of black paint.

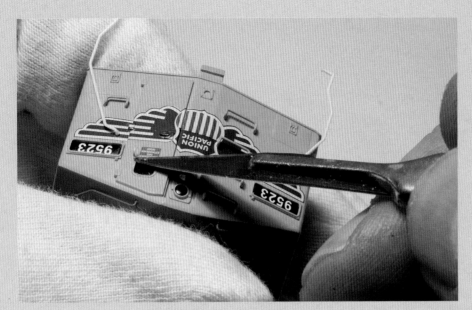

Before applying the weathering

I trimmed off the lip around the window with a sharp scalpel. Wearing the white glove prevents leaving any fingerprints on the nose.

Next, I cut a piece of styrene to fit the window opening and glued it in place flush with the door. I matched the locomotive's yellow using Humbrol 154 with a tiny bit of 70 added to it. You can still see where the window used to be. The UP welded a metal plate in the opening, and it is visible on the real locomotives too.

I have also added a Details West GPS dome to the cab roof, which I have seen on a few of UP's Dash 8-40CWs.

Windows and number boards were masked before the airbrushing. Main head and ditch lights received a dab of liquid mask (Humbrol Maskol).

Note the headlight is yellow and not silver. Judging from my photos, this is prototypically correct. The headlights apparently were not masked when the locomotives were repainted.

The wheel wipers were masked with small pieces of masking tape to prevent paint from interfering with the electrical pickup. The motor and everything else mounted in the frame was wrapped in masking tape.

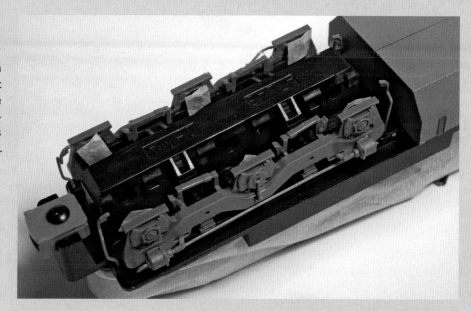

Now the actual weathering can begin. To add some depth to grilles and air intakes, I gave them a black wash. I used black Vallejo Air right out of the bottle for this.

When the black paint was dry, I scraped the top of the grilles with a scalpel, again being careful not the scrape off any of the underlying colors.

A quick light weathering

To simulate the dust found on the roof and walkways, I gave them a coat of sand color thinned to a wash. This also leaves a flat surface excellent for receiving powdered chalks.

Some soot went onto the roof in the form of black powdered chalks applied with a soft brush. The areas around the exhaust received the most with less toward the ends.

The lower areas received some road grime with an airbrush application of Model Master Dark Skintone thinned to a wash.

Finally everything was sealed with a coat of Vallejo Satin Varnish.

The more heavily weathered SD60M leading the train is much dirtier than the trailing AC4400W.

I masked the windows and number boards with masking tape. Head and ditch lights received a dab of liquid Humbrol Maskol. The wheel wipers were masked to prevent paint from interfering with the electrical pick up. Now the actual weathering can begin. I started by giving all grilles and air intakes a black wash to give them some depth. I used black Vallejo Air right out of the bottle for this but you can use any type of black paint thinned to the consistency of a wash.

When the black paint was dry, I scraped the top of the grilles with a scalpel. Be careful not to scrape off any of the locomotive's colors. Upper flat surfaces are usually lighter because of dust that settles there. To lighten the roof and walkways, I gave them a coat of sand thinned to a wash. This also leaves a flat surface excellent for receiving powdered chalks.

The roof received some soot around the exhaust, thinning the grime toward both ends in the form of black powdered chalks applied with a soft brush.

The lower areas received some road grime. For this, I used Model Master Dark Skintone thinned almost to a wash, which completed the light weathering.

Everything was sealed with a coat of clear varnish. I used Vallejo Satin Varnish because this model represented a newly repainted unit. Had it been a locomotive with older paint, I would have used Vallejo Flat finish instead.

Finally, the wheel sides received Model Master Dark Skintone applied with a brush, and the model was ready to assemble and be put on the track.

Apply DCC and sound
to an older Kato SD70MAC

A couple of years ago I was bitten by the sound bug and wanted to equip all my locomotives with sound. I experimented with different types of decoders and settled on ESU LokSound decoders because they seemed to work best with my Lenz DCC system. The sound of the LokSound decoders was also among the best I've heard. ESU offers a large variety of sound files you can download from the company's website and install via its Lok Programmer.

Nowadays most non-sound equipped HO scale locomotives have room for a speaker because the same locomotive is offered with sound too. However, many of my older locomotives date from a time before sound was common, and there's not much room left for a speaker. In order to have sound in these older units, I would have to make some space for it.

The round speaker and cabinet packaged with the LokSound decoder was too wide to fit inside the shell if placed in its intended horizontal position. I figured it would be too much work to make room for the speaker in the fuel tank. Instead I placed the speaker diagonally inside the

shell toward the rear of the locomotive. This required a custom-built speaker cabinet, although that was relatively easy to make. Even so, I had to remove a part of the frame to make room for a speaker.

The lights also needed some modification. As standard, the ditch lights and headlights are illuminated by the same LED. I wanted to change that so I could turn on the head and ditch lights individually.

The LEDs for the front and rear light are both attached to the circuit board above the motor. The lights' leads are then threaded to the front and rear lights

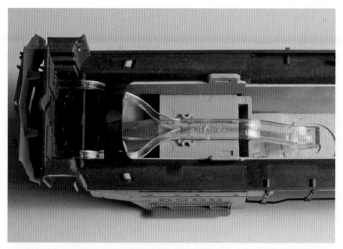

All the lights in the front are illuminated using the same LED. This had to be changed so the headlights and ditch lights could be turned on and off individually.

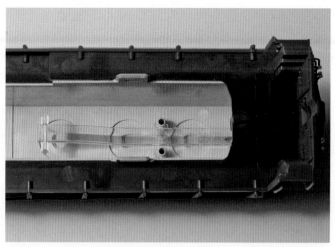

The clear plastic optic leading to the rear light was in the way of the speaker cabinet and had to be trimmed to allow clearance.

through clear plastic optics. I shortened the ditch light piece and attached a separate LED to it. I wrapped aluminum foil around the plastic optic to prevent light from shining through the headlight section and visa versa.

The plastic optic leading to the rear light had to be shortened as much as possible to make room for the speaker. I cut off the rear LED from the circuit board and moved it to the back of the locomotive. It was then attached into the hole I had drilled in the optic.

I drilled a hole in the clear plastic optic for the LED as close to the rear headlights as possible.

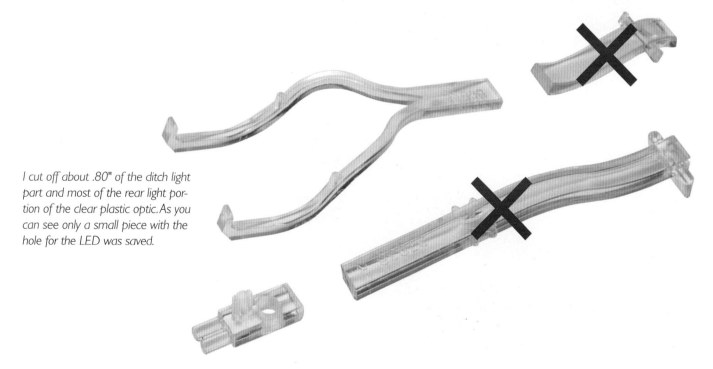

I cut off about .80" of the ditch light part and most of the rear light portion of the clear plastic optic. As you can see only a small piece with the hole for the LED was saved.

Installing light and sound

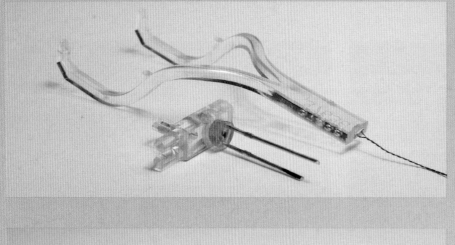

I snapped off the rear LED from the circuit board and pressed it into the hole I drilled in the shortened plastic optic. A micro LED was attached to the end of the ditch light assembly with Micro Kristal Klear.

The ditch light system sits on top of the headlight system, so I wrapped the end of the ditch light system with aluminum foil to prevent any light from the headlight from shining through the ditch lights and vice versa.

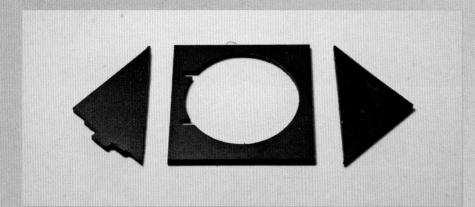

The round speaker that comes with the ESU LokSound decoder is too wide for a horizontal placement. Instead I set it diagonally in a custom-made speaker cabinet.

The cabinet is glued in place. To seal all joints, I gave them an extra layer of glue to make sure the cabinet was completely airtight. If air can escape the cabinet, the speaker will not create pleasing sound.

Note the rear light assembly is also wrapped with aluminum foil to prevent any light from shining through the plastic shell.

I had to remove a corner of the metal
frame to make room for the speaker.
I cut it with a rotary motor tool. I
covered the gear mechanism with tape
to protect it from the metal dust caused
by the cutting.

Here is a close-up of the circuit board.
Kato has prepared two holes where
you can attach the wires for the AUX 1
output, which in this case are the ditch
lights. A 4.7K ohm resistor is needed
between the LED for the ditch lights
and the decoder output's common wire
and the LED's + wire (A). The other
wire is soldered to the attachment
connected to the decoder's green wire
(B). To the right, you can see where
the LED for the rear light used to be
attached but has been replaced with
extension wires.

Below you can see the complete
installation with decoder and speaker.
To create an airtight seal, the speaker is
glued to the cabinet with silicone glue.

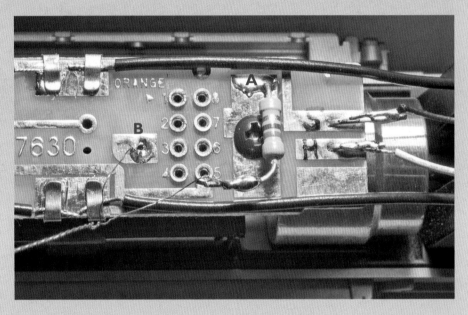

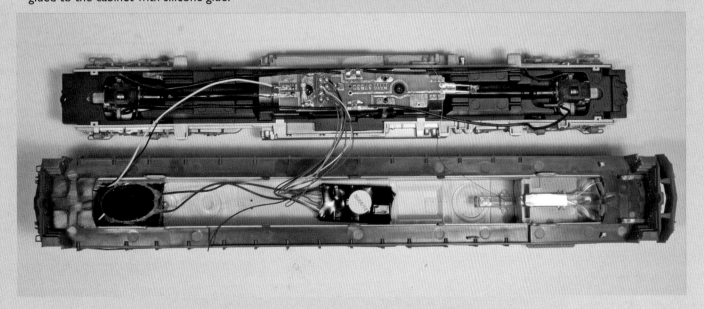

Apply a multi-color paint scheme to an undecorated Kato GP35

Painting and detailing undecorated locomotive models have almost become lost arts as a result of the selection of well-detailed models offered on the market today. About the only times you might be interested in a complete new livery would be to model a freelanced railroad or if you just want a rare paint scheme not offered commercially.

I have had an old undecorated Kato GP35 sitting on my hobby shelf for years. Originally I planned to detail and decorate it as a Santa Fe unit, but when Santa Fe merged with BN, I decided to wait and

see what paint scheme they settled on. The years passed without any progress on the project. Then recently I picked up a new client for my graphic arts business. BLDX is a locomotive leasing company based in Denmark. I designed a new logo for the company and so was also involved in developing a new paint scheme for its locomotives.

So I thought it would be fun to paint a locomotive for my layout in BLDX's new colors and new logo. Finally, my GP35 had a good reason to come out of the box after 12 years on the shelf.

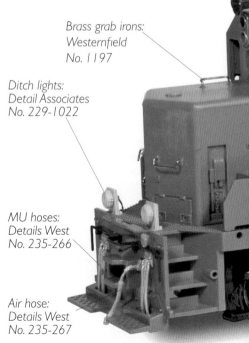

"Firecracker" antenna:
Details West No. 235-157

Brass grab irons:
Westernfield
No. 1197

Ditch lights:
Detail Associates
No. 229-1022

MU hoses:
Details West
No. 235-266

Air hose:
Details West
No. 235-267

I had no specific prototype to follow, as the BLDX locomotives are all Danish prototypes and all are very different from U.S. prototypes.

You probably do not want to model this fictitious BLDX locomotive, but you can use the same techniques for detailing and applying a multi-color paint scheme on any other diesel locomotive.

Adding a few extra details to the model

The most basic detail parts were supplied with the Kato model, but it lacked details such as m.u. hoses, cab sunshades, and ditch lights. For my model, I replaced the plastic add-on grab irons with wire grab irons. And for crew comfort, I added an air conditioner to the cab roof.

For ditch lights, I used Details Associates No. 1022. I glued the light casting to the stand and drilled a hole through the

lamp. A micro LED was attached to the backside of each of the ditch lights, and the ditch lights were mounted on the front deck with glue. I drilled a hole in the deck behind each of the ditch lights for the wires coming from the LEDs.

Painting the parts

I used acrylic paint for this project. My favorite brand is Vallejo Air, which comes ready for your airbrush directly from the bottle—no thinning necessary. They dry fast, and you can apply a mask on a newly painted surface after just 15 minutes.

Vallejo's line-up is primarily military colors, but the company also offers basic colors such as yellow, red, blue, green, and of course black and white. With these colors, you can mix nearly any shade of color you wish.

I separated the model into as many pieces as possible for painting. All the

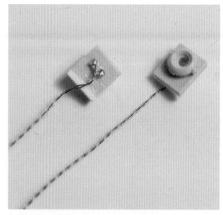

The ditch lights were from Details Associates and illuminated by micro LEDs.

parts were scrubbed with hot water and household detergent. I used an old toothbrush for this job. From there on, I was very careful not to touch any of the surfaces that would receive paint Even the slightest touch from our fingers can leave skin oils, which will cause the paint not to stick properly to the model. Solvent-based paints are a bit more tolerant than water-

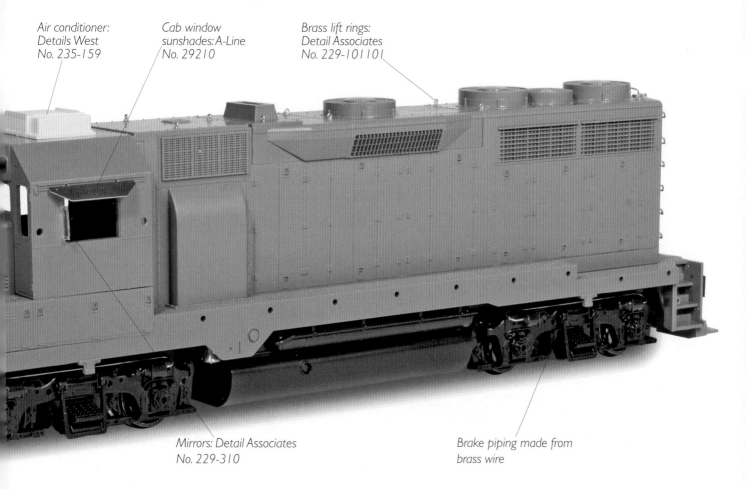

Air conditioner:
Details West
No. 235-159

Cab window
sunshades: A-Line
No. 29210

Brass lift rings:
Detail Associates
No. 229-101101

Mirrors: Detail Associates
No. 229-310

Brake piping made from
brass wire

Painting a locomotive

Before I applied any paint, I scrubbed all parts in hot water with a few drops of household detergent added to it. I blew off as much of the water as possible with my airbrush. When the parts were completely dry, I gave everything a neutral-gray base coat.

Then I applied the first color. Always start with the lightest color. In this case, it was white, which I applied in several light coats.

The areas that were supposed to remain white were masked with masking tape. The Vallejo paint dries very fast, so you can apply masking tape on a newly painted surface after just 15 minutes. I rubbed all edges down to make sure that no paint could slip under the masking when the next color was applied.

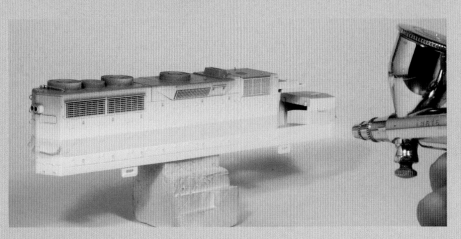

The light green was applied to the hood, walkways, and handrails. The lighter the color, the more layers it takes for it to cover, so this green took several coats.

I masked the light green area and sprayed the hood, cab, and tank with dark green.

Metallic colors cover extremely well, so these trucks only required a single coat of silver.

I removed the masking immediately after the last coat of paint was applied. The best way to avoid tearing any paint off is to pull the masking tape back at an angle.

The yellow stripe that separates the white and green areas was made from a decal. I trimmed off clear decal film around the stripes and dipped the decal in water. A decal setting solution was applied along the edge of the white area. Slide the stripe in place. Try to place it as precisely as possible. If you need to adjust the stripe, apply more setting solution to the area and push it gently in place with a soft brush. Finally, apply a little Solvaset to the stripe. This will soften the decal and make it look as if it has been painted on.

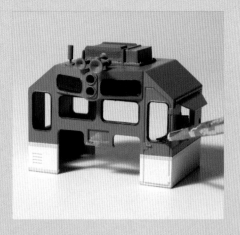 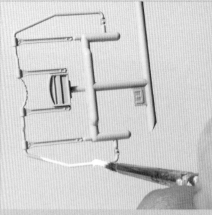

All smaller details like the black window gaskets, MU hoses, number boards, white step edges, and corner handrails were painted with a fine brush.

The decals were made from my design by a modeling club that has invested in a printer, but you could find custom decal makers through an Internet search. I trimmed off as much of the clear decal film around the decals as possible before applying them. I wetted the area where the decal was to be applied with Micro Set and slid the decal in place. Then I brushed Solvaset on top of the decal. This softens it and enables it to snuggle down over hinges and seams so it looks painted-on when dry.

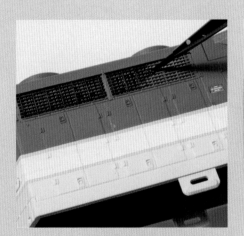 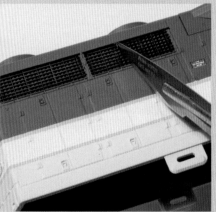

To give the grilles depth, they received a black wash. I used a black Vallejo Air right out of the bottle for this. The Vallejo Air paints are so thin that they almost look like a wash. When the black paint was dry, I gently scrape the top of the grilles with a scalpel till the green paint was visible.

The roof received some soot in the form of black powdered chalks applied with a soft brush. Road grime on lower areas is Model Master Dark Skintone thinned to a wash and applied with an airbrush.

Finally everything was sealed with a coat of Vallejo Satin Varnish.

based paints, which are especially sensitive to finger oil.

As you can see on the picture on page 81, the body shell was gray, the tank and horn were black, and other detail parts were either white or bare metal. In order to create a uniform undercoat to help render the BLDX colors accurately, I first airbrushed all parts with a neutral gray.

Then I applied the colors one by one starting with the lightest color, which in this case was white. The white area was masked and the light green was applied, then the light green area was then masked and the dark green was applied.

I used a fine brush to paint all smaller details like the window gaskets, number boards, step edges, corner handrails, MU hoses, and others.

The yellow stripe that separates the white and green areas was made from a decal. I trimmed off the clear decal film around the stripes before applying them. The company logo and road numbers came from a custom-made decal sheet.

The model only received a light weathering as it was supposed to look like a recently repainted locomotive. The weathering included soot on the roof and road grime on the lower areas. I reassembled the model partially before weathering it, and sealed with Vallejo Satin Varnish.

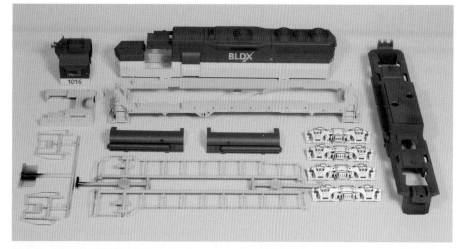

The model was separated into as many pieces as possible for painting.

DCC and sound

The model dates from a time when the term "DCC ready" didn't exist, so I had to prepare it for DCC and sound.

I trimmed off a part of the frame to make room for a speaker. While I had out the saw, I modified the head and rear lights by trimming the clear plastic optics as described in the previous chapter and replacing the light bulbs with LEDs.

Horn hook couplers were the norm when I bought this locomotive, so I replaced them with a pair of Kadee's scale couplers.

Don't forget to paint the wheels. I gave them a grimy brownish color.

Index

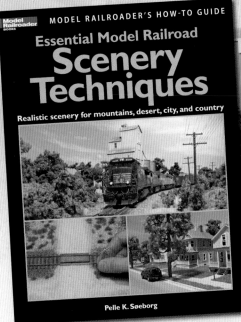
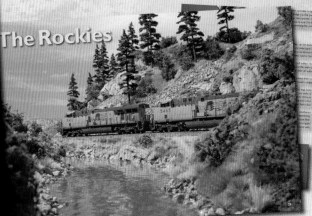

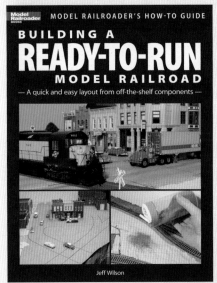

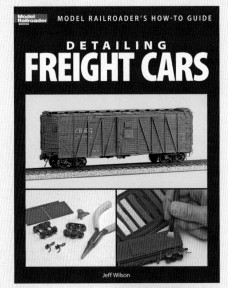

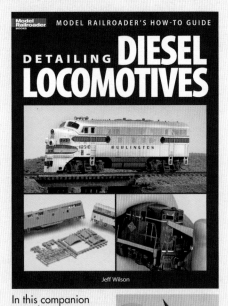